We love you,
Aunt Jean

Lynda
&
Phil

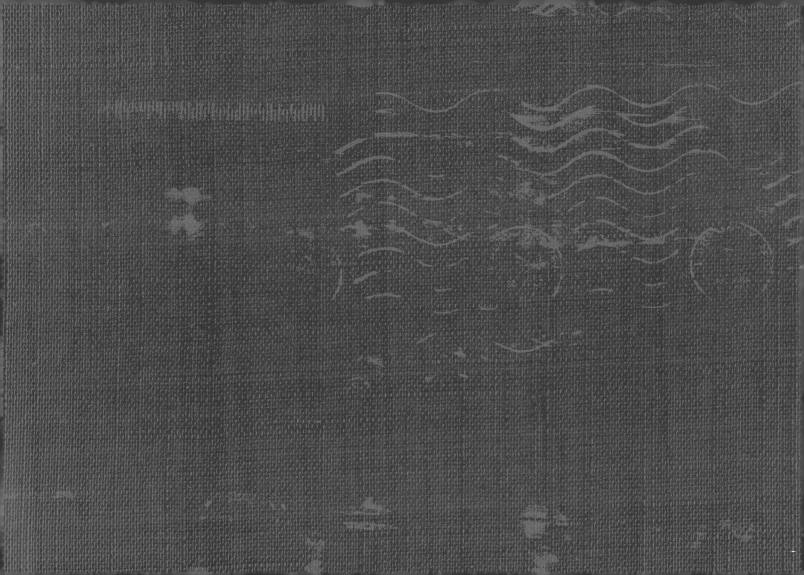

TO

_____

FROM

_____

You Are Loved

© 2012 by Thomas Nelson, Inc.

Published in Nashville, Tennessee, by Thomas Nelson®. Thomas Nelson is a trademark of Thomas Nelson, Inc.

Compiled by Karen Moore.

Project managed by Michelle Prater Burke.

Cover and interior design by Thinkpen Design, Inc., www.thinkpendesign.com

Thomas Nelson, Inc., titles may be purchased in bulk for educational, business, fund-raising, or sales promotional use. For information, please e-mail SpecialMarkets@ThomasNelson.com.

Grateful acknowledgment is made to all quoted authors and to the following publishers and copyright holders: **C. D. Baker**, taken from *101 Cups of Water*. Colorado Springs, CO: WaterBrook Press, © 2008. **Robert Brault**, taken from robertbrault.com. **John Eldredge**, taken from *Dare to Desire*. Nashville, TN: Thomas Nelson, Inc., © 2002 by John Eldredge. **Richard J. Foster**, taken from *Prayer: Finding the Heart's True Home*. New York: HarperCollins, © 1992 by Richard J. Foster. **Billy Graham**, taken from *The Journey*. Nashville, TN: Thomas Nelson, Inc., © 2006 by Billy Graham. **Max Lucado**, taken from *God Thinks You're Wonderful!* Nashville, TN: Thomas Nelson, Inc., © 2003 by Max Lucado; and taken from *Grace for the Moment*. Nashville, TN: Thomas Nelson, Inc., © 2009 by Max Lucado. **Karl Menninger**, taken from *A Psychiatrist's World*. New York: Viking Press, © 1959. **Donald Miller**, taken from *Blue Like Jazz*. Nashville, TN: Thomas Nelson, Inc., © 2003 by Donald Miller. **Sheila Walsh**, taken from *God Has a Dream for Your Life*. Nashville, TN: Thomas Nelson, Inc., © 2006 by Sheila Walsh.

Unless otherwise noted, Scripture quotations are taken from The New King James Version. © 1982, 1992 by Thomas Nelson, Inc. Used by permission. All rights reserved. Scripture quotations marked CEV are from The Contemporary English Version. © 1991 by the American Bible Society. Used by permission. Those marked ESV are taken from The English Standard Version. © 2001 by Crossway Bibles, a division of Good News Publishers. Used by permission. Those marked NCV are from New Century Version ®. © 2005 by Thomas Nelson, Inc. Used by permission. All rights reserved. Those marked NIV are from Holy Bible: New International Version ®. © 1973, 1978, 1984 by International Bible Society. Used by permission of Zondervan Publishing House. All rights reserved. Those marked NLT are from Holy Bible, New Living Translation. © 1996. Used by permission of Tyndale House Publishers, Inc., Wheaton, Illinois 60189. All rights reserved.

ISBN-13: 978-1-4003-1837-7

Printed in China.

13 14 15 LEO 5 4 3 2

www.thomasnelson.com

SIMPLE REMINDERS OF GOD'S LOVE AND MINE

YOU ARE *Loved*

THOMAS NELSON
Since 1798

NASHVILLE   DALLAS   MEXICO CITY   RIO DE JANEIRO

We love because God
first loved us.

You are always loved, always treasured, always blessed.

You cannot touch love . . . , but you can feel the sweetness it pours into everything.

HELEN KELLER

Nothing is sweeter than love, nothing stronger,
nothing higher, nothing wider, nothing more pleasant,
nothing fuller or better in heaven or earth.

THOMAS À KEMPIS

The love we give away is the only love we keep.

ELBERT HUBBARD

You will find as you look back upon your life that the moments when you really lived are the moments when you have done things in the spirit of love.

HENRY DRUMMOND

Follow the way of love.

1 CORINTHIANS 14:1 NIV

Love doesn't make the world go 'round.
Love is what makes the ride worthwhile.

FRANKLIN P. JONES

Love began with the One who perfectly
designed you to love and be loved; . . .

. . . love grows with those who treasure you now and those who are yet to be blessed by knowing you.

Those who love deeply
never grow old; they
may die of old age,
but they die young.

SIR ARTHUR PINERO

To find someone who will love you for no reason, and to shower that person with reasons, that is the ultimate happiness.

ROBERT BRAULT

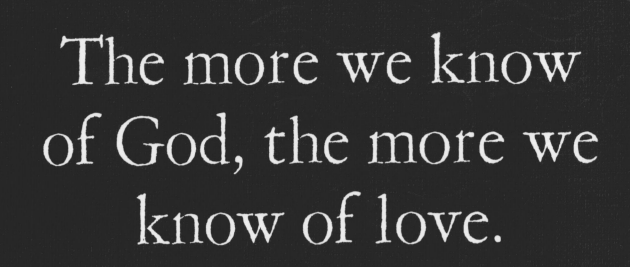

The more we know of God, the more we know of love.

Faith, like light, should always be simple and unbending;
while love, like warmth, should beam forth on every side.

MARTIN LUTHER

The secret of your life is written on your heart's desire.

JOHN ELDREDGE

Be of good comfort, be of one mind, live in peace; and the God of love and peace will be with you.

2 CORINTHIANS 13:11

The ones you love
in your heart are but
guests in your soul.

JIM COTTER

One word frees us of all the weight
and pain of life. That word is *love*.

SOPHOCLES

You are a twinkle of light in the darkness.

The God of the universe, the one who holds the stars and the moon in place, knows everything about you and loves you with unprecedented abandon.

SHEILA WALSH

Love is a great beautifier.

LOUISA MAY ALCOTT

Our Lord does not care so much for
the importance of our works as for
the love with which they are done.

TERESA OF AVILA

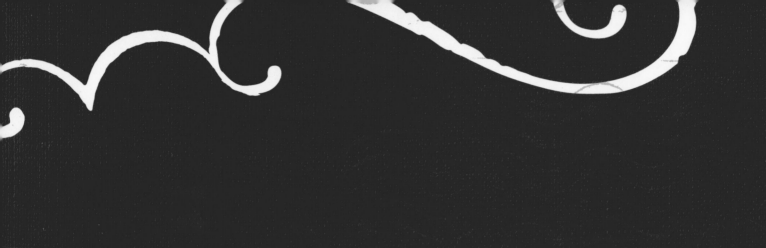

You make God smile.

For true love is inexhaustible; the
more you give, the more you have.

ANTOINE DE SAINT-EXUPÉRY

Love cures people, both the ones who give it and the ones who receive it.

KARL MENNINGER

A blessed thing it is for any man or woman to have a friend, one human soul whom we can trust utterly, who knows the best and worst of us, and who loves us in spite of all our faults.

CHARLES KINGSLEY

We are tied to each
other by heartstrings.

A parent's love is whole no matter
how many times divided.

ROBERT BRAULT

You're simply awesome!

Think how much the Father loves us.
He loves us so much that He lets us be
called His children, as we truly are.

1 JOHN 3:1 CEV

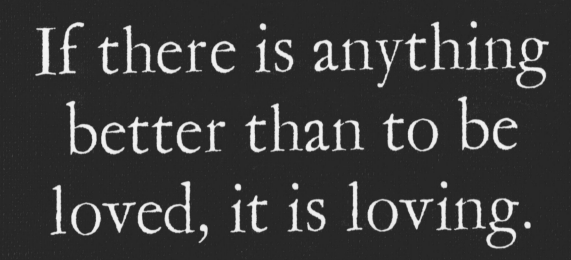

If there is anything
better than to be
loved, it is loving.

ANONYMOUS

Neither a lofty degree of intelligence nor imagination nor both together go to the making of genius. Love, love, love – that is the soul of genius.

WOLFGANG AMADEUS MOZART

God thinks you're wonderful!

MAX LUCADO

For the LORD your God is living among you. . . .
With His love, He will calm all your fears.

ZEPHANIAH 3:17 NLT

Friends don't notice the miles that separate them. Their connection is sealed with a love that nothing can change.

A new commandment I give to you, that
you love one another; as I have loved
you, that you also love one another.

JOHN 13:34

I have loved you with an everlasting love.

JEREMIAH 31:3

The love of the Father is like a sudden rain shower
that will pour forth when you least expect it,
catching you up into wonder and praise.

RICHARD J. FOSTER

You don't touch love;
love touches you.

Love is a fruit in season at all times, and within reach of every hand. Anyone may gather it, and no limit is set.

MOTHER TERESA

God loves you just
the way you are, but
He refuses to leave
you that way.

MAX LUCADO

We know that God is always at work for
the good of everyone who loves him.

You're on a first-name basis with the King of the universe.

If love surrounds us, God surrounds us.

C. D. BAKER

Many waters cannot quench love, nor can the floods drown it.

SONG OF SOLOMON 8:7

Love ever gives, forgives, outlives . . .
and ever stands with open hands.

JOHN OXENHAM

You are beautiful!

SONG OF SOLOMON 7:6 CEV

You aren't loved because you're valuable.
You're valuable because God loves you.

ANONYMOUS

There is no surprise more magical than the surprise of being loved. It is God's finger on man's shoulder.

CHARLES MORGAN

In everything we have won more than a victory because of Christ who loves us. I am sure that nothing can separate us from God's love.

ROMANS 8:37-38 CEV

You are as prone to love
as the sun is to shine.

THOMAS TRAHERNE

Love holds the questions close to the
heart and quietly awaits the answers.

If I loved you less,
I might be able to talk
about it more.

JANE AUSTEN

Love is both something that happens to
you and something you decide upon.

DONALD MILLER

Love is the beauty of the soul.

ST. AUGUSTINE

Love bears all things, believes all things,
hopes all things, endures all things.

1 CORINTHIANS 13:7 ESV

God's love . . . is a profound and unshakable
commitment that seeks what is best for us; . . .

. . . human love may change or fade. God's love never will.

BILLY GRAHAM

A loving heart is the truest wisdom.

CHARLES DICKENS

Love feels no burden, thinks nothing of trouble, attempts what is above its strength, pleads no excuse of impossibility; for it thinks . . . all things possible.

THOMAS À KEMPIS

I have loved you, just as my Father has loved me. So remain faithful to my love for you.

JOHN 15:9 CEV